D0855030

Trapdoor Spiders

by Claire Archer

Visit us at www.abdopublishing.com

Published by Abdo Kids, a division of ABDO, PO Box 398166, Minneapolis, Minnesota 55439.

Copyright © 2015 by Abdo Consulting Group, Inc. International copyrights reserved in all countries. No part of this book may be reproduced in any form without written permission from the publisher.

Printed in the United States of America, North Mankato, Minnesota.

032014

092014

 PRINTED ON RECYCLED PAPER

Photo Credits: Getty Images, Minden Pictures, Shutterstock, SuperStock

Production Contributors: Teddy Borth, Jennie Forsberg, Grace Hansen

Design Contributors: Dorothy Toth, Laura Rask

Library of Congress Control Number: 2013952995

Cataloging-in-Publication Data

Archer, Claire.

 Trapdoor spiders / Claire Archer.

   p. cm. -- (Spiders)

ISBN 978-1-62970-075-5 (lib. bdg.)

Includes bibliographical references and index.

1. Trapdoor spiders--Juvenile literature.   I. Title.

595.4--dc23

2013952995

Table of Contents

Trapdoor Spiders

Trapdoor spiders can be found all over the world. They mainly live in warm **climates**.

5

Trapdoor spiders are usually brown or black. Some are reddish. Females are larger than males.

Trapdoor spiders have eight legs. They also have eight eyes!

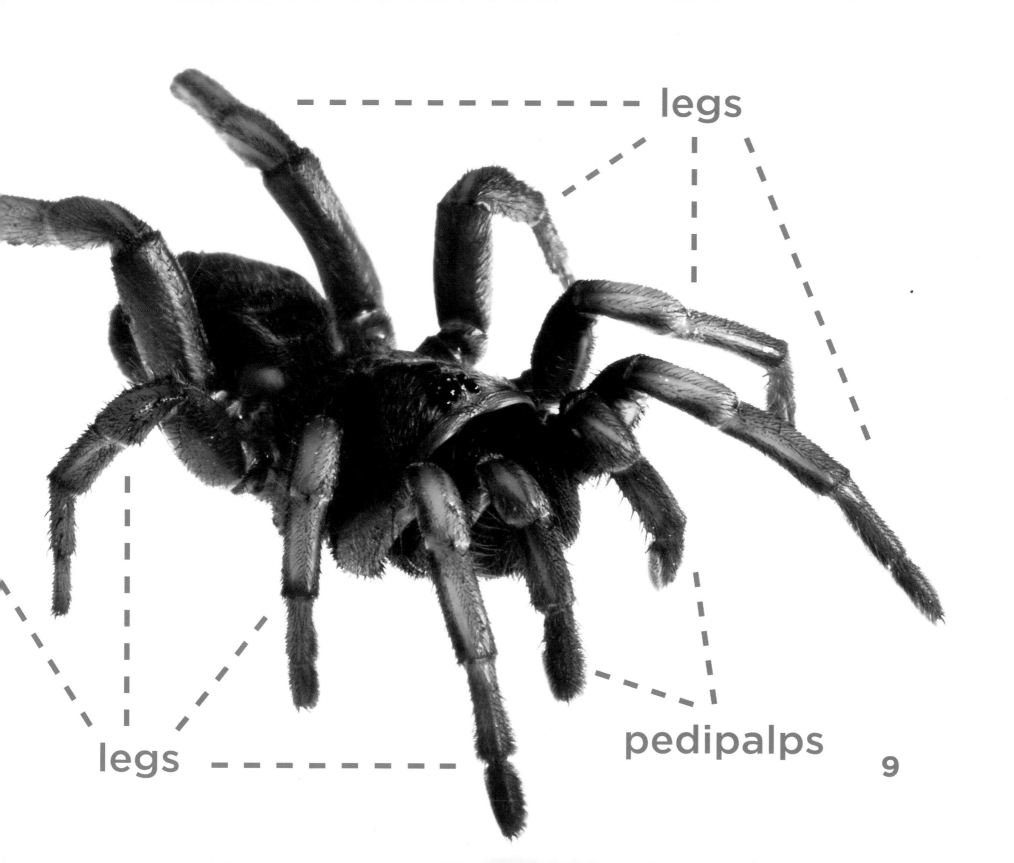

legs

legs

pedipalps

9

Trapdoor spiders get their name from their homes. They live in **burrows** with trapdoors.

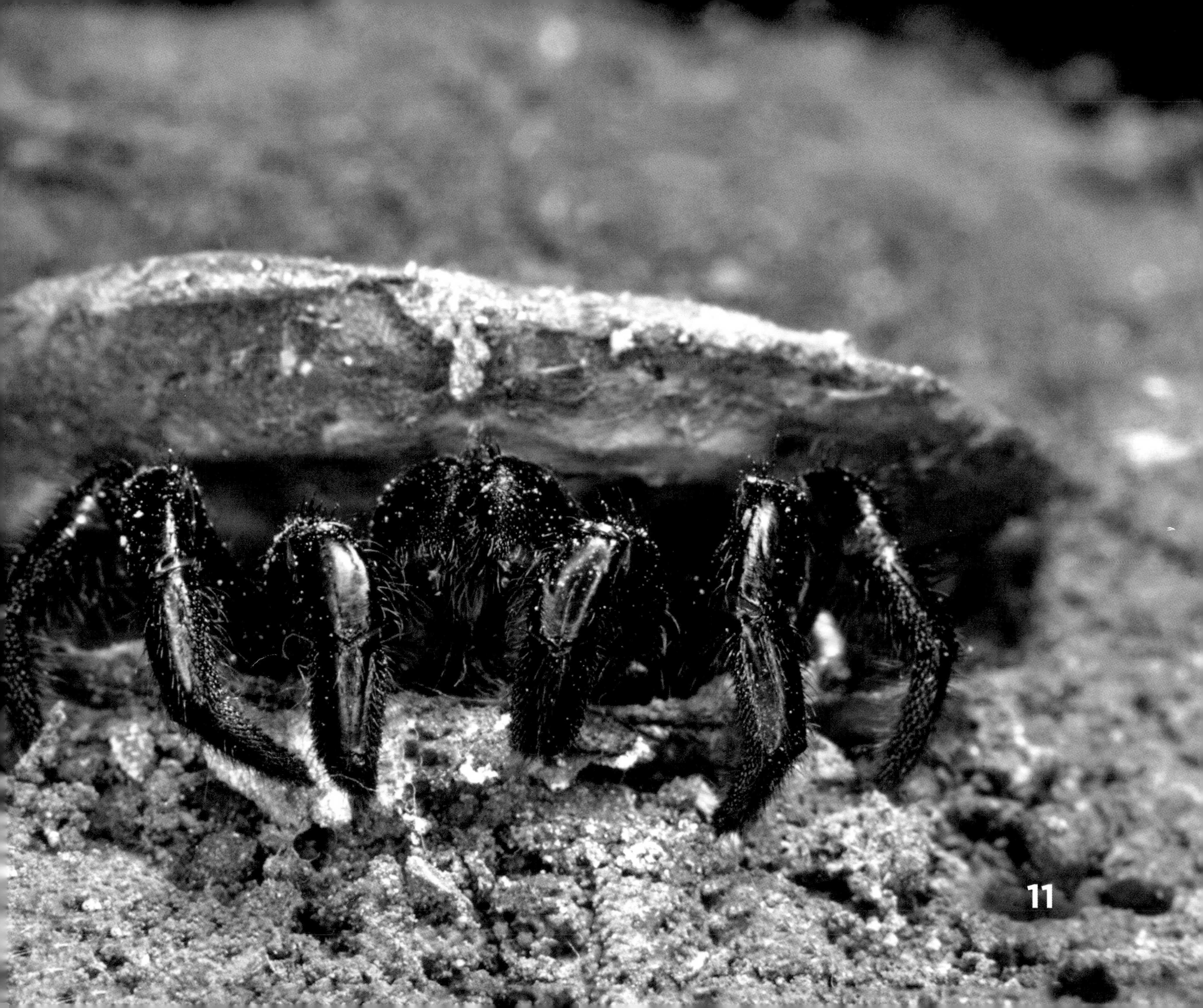

Trapdoor spiders dig their **burrow** homes. Then they line their burrows with silk.

12

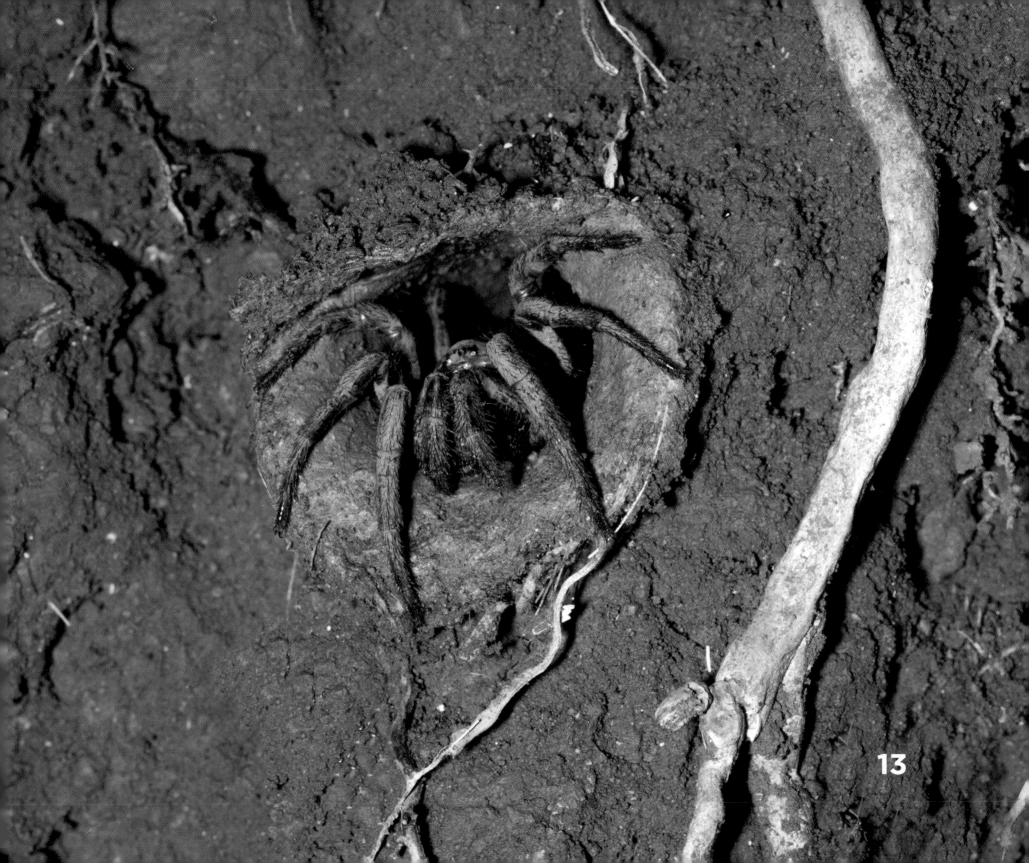

13

Hunting

Trapdoor spiders wait in their **burrows**. They feel the **vibrations** of **prey** walking by.

The trapdoor spider pops out of its **burrow**. It grabs its **prey**. It pulls its prey into the burrow.

The trapdoor spider then bites its prey. It injects venom into its prey.

19

Food

Trapdoor spiders eat many different insects. They even eat lizards, frogs, and mice!

More Facts

- Female trapdoor spiders spend most of their time underground in their homes. Males are more likely to venture out of their homes.

- Young trapdoor spiders will stay in the **burrow** with their mother for several months.

- Trapdoor spiders are closely related to tarantulas.

Glossary

burrow – an animal's underground home.

climate – the weather and temperatures that are normal in a certain place.

pedipalps - feelers on a spider's face that helps it sense, grab, and hold onto prey.

prey – an animal hunted or killed by a predator for food.

venom – a poison made by some animals and insects. It usually enters a victim through a bite or a sting.

vibration – tiny back and forth movements.

Index

abdokids.com

Use this code to log on to abdokids.com and access crafts, games, videos and more!

Abdo Kids Code:
STK0755